Low Sodium, Low Carb Cookbook:

Delicious Recipes for a Healthy and Balanced Diet

Benjamin Abby

Copyright © 2023, Benjamin Abby

Dear Reader,

Thank you for your reading this book.

If you have any questions, suggestions or would like to contact me, please send an email at **babby2719@gmail.com**.

I look forward to hearing from you!

Sincerely,

Benjamin Abby

THANK YOU

TABLE OF CONTENTS

INTRODUCTION

Welcome

This book was intended to present you with tasty, wholesome, and easy-to-prepare meals that help you keep a healthy lifestyle.

Whether you are wanting to minimize your salt consumption or cut down on carbohydrates, this cookbook offers something for you.

It features more than 40 recipes that are both low in salt and low in carbs that are guaranteed to tickle your taste buds.

We have included recipes for breakfast, lunch, supper, and snacks so that you can quickly find something that meets your requirements.

All of the recipes are simple to follow and contain extensive instructions on how to cook them.

We recognize that it might be challenging to discover meals that are both low in salt and low in carbs.

That is why we have put up this cookbook and have included all of the relevant nutritional information for each dish.

Each dish has been created to be both nutritional and enjoyable. We have reduced the components to a minimum and have utilized natural and healthful products wherever feasible.

We have also taken into mind your dietary preferences by offering gluten-free and dairy-free alternatives.

We hope that you discover something that you appreciate in this cookbook. We have attempted to make this book as user-friendly as possible and have added useful tips and pointers throughout. So, what are you waiting for?

Let's begin cooking!

We recognize that maintaining a healthy lifestyle may be tough, particularly with all of the harmful food options out there.

That is why we have designed this cookbook to help you make the proper decisions. We are convinced that you will discover something that you appreciate in this cookbook and that it will assist you to eat healthier and feel better.

We hope you like this Cookbook and find it useful in making good living choices.

Happy cooking!

CHAPTER 1

Getting Started with Low Sodium Low Carb Cooking

1.1 What is a Low Sodium Low Carb Diet?

A low sodium low carb diet is a dietary plan that is aimed to help minimize the quantity of salt and carbohydrates in your diet.

This sort of diet is excellent for patients who have high blood pressure, diabetes, renal illness, and heart disease.

It is also good for individuals who are attempting to reduce weight.

The major emphasis of a low sodium low carb diet is to limit the quantity of salt and carbs you ingest.

This may help to minimize your chance of developing health issues connected with high blood pressure, diabetes, and heart disease. It may also assist to lower your body weight.

This sort of diet is also useful for persons who wish to maintain a healthy weight.

To follow a low sodium low carb diet, you must minimize the quantity of salt and carbs you ingest. This involves avoiding processed meals, fast food, and other high-sodium items.

You should also avoid items that are rich in sugar, such as candies, cakes, and cookies. Instead, concentrate on consuming foods that are strong in fiber and protein, such as lean meats, fish, eggs, and legumes.

In terms of carbs, a low sodium low carb diet demands restricting your consumption of white flour, white rice, potatoes, and other starchy grains.

Instead, concentrate on ingesting whole-grain slices of bread and pasta, as well as vegetables and fruits.

You should also restrict your consumption of processed carbs, such as cakes, cookies, and sweetened drinks.

When it comes to sodium, you should minimize your consumption of table salt, as well as processed and canned foods.

Instead, choose fresh, unprocessed foods and utilize herbs, spices, and other low-sodium ingredients to flavor your meals. You should avoid adding extra salt to your meals.

In addition to minimizing your consumption of salt and carbs, you should also concentrate on consuming a variety of healthful meals.

This contains a mix of lean proteins, healthy fats, and complex carbs. Eating a variety of meals may assist to ensure that you are receiving all the vital nutrients your body requires.

Following a low salt low carb diet might be tough. It is crucial to pay great attention to the food labels while grocery shopping and to check the nutrition data on packaged goods.

You should try to plan out your meals in advance to ensure that you are consuming the right balance of nutrients each day.

Overall, a low-salt low-carb diet may be good for persons who wish to lower their risk of developing health issues related to **high blood pressure, diabetes,** and **heart disease**.

It may also be good for people who are attempting to shed or maintain a healthy weight.

By reducing your consumption of salt and carbs and concentrating on eating a variety of nutritious meals, you may boost your chances of accomplishing your health and weight reduction objectives.

A low sodium low carb diet is a dietary plan that is aimed to help minimize the quantity of salt and carbohydrates in your diet.

This sort of diet may be useful for persons who have high blood pressure, diabetes, renal illness, and heart disease, or who are attempting to reduce weight.

By reducing your consumption of salt and carbs and concentrating on eating a variety of nutritious meals, you may boost your chances of accomplishing your health and weight reduction objectives.

1.2 Benefits of a Low Sodium Low Carb Diet

A low-sodium low-carb diet is a dietary program that restricts the consumption of foods that are rich in salt and carbs.

This sort of diet has been more popular in recent years as individuals attempt to shed weight and enhance their general health.

There are several advantages to adopting a low salt low-carb diet, including weight reduction, reduced blood pressure, and lower cholesterol levels.

Weight reduction: One of the key advantages of a low salt low-carb diet is weight reduction. By restricting your consumption of salt and carbs, your body can burn more fat, resulting in weight reduction.

A low-sodium low-carb diet may help you lose weight in a healthy and lasting manner. Additionally, this type of diet is low in calories, which can help you maintain your weight loss in the long term.

Better Blood Pressure: A low salt low carb diet may help improve your blood pressure. Sodium is known to elevate blood pressure, and a low-sodium diet may help minimize your risk of hypertension.

A low-carb diet might lower your risk of developing diabetes, which is an issue that can cause high blood pressure.

Improved Cholesterol Levels: A low salt low carb diet may also aid to enhance your cholesterol levels.

By lowering your consumption of salt and carbs, you may decrease your levels of **"bad"** cholesterol, which can lessen your chance of developing heart disease.

A low sodium low carb diet can help to reduce your levels of triglycerides, which is another type of fat that can lead to heart disease.

Improved Digestive Health: A low salt low carb diet may also assist to enhance your digestive health. By avoiding meals that are heavy in salt and carbs, you may minimize your chance of experiencing digestive disorders including constipation, diarrhea, and gas.

A low sodium low carb diet can help boost your overall gut health, which may result in better digestion and absorption of nutrients.

Improved Mental Health: A low salt low carb diet may also assist to enhance your mental health. By avoiding meals that are heavy in salt and carbs, you may minimize your chance of experiencing sadness and anxiety.

A low sodium low carb diet also can help to improve your cognitive function, which can lead to improved mental clarity and focus.

A reduced sodium low carb diet can offer many health benefits. By avoiding meals that are heavy in salt and carbs, you may minimize your chance of acquiring a range of health concerns.

Low sodium low carb diet can help you lose weight and improve your overall health.

For people who are trying to enhance their health and reduce weight, a low-sodium low-carb diet may be the right option.

This sort of diet may help you attain your health objectives safely and sustainably.

1.3 Tips for Getting Started

Dieting isn't easy. But consuming low carbs should not be the reason. I want you to have the same success I've achieved.

The early few days of any new method of eating might be a bit daunting. This is a vital handbook for anybody new to the world of low-carb living.

It will provide you with everything you need to know, from how to establish goals, measure your progress, make tasty meals and take action to maximize your health.

It starts by outlining **10 helpful recommendations** on how to achieve success on the Low Carb Process.

Don't Do It Alone

Kick-starting a new diet may be difficult, particularly if you are going at it alone. There are so many advantages to utilizing a support network or finding a diet companion.

Not only can you share your experience and success, but you can also trade ideas and advice and be there during challenging times.

Don't worry if your friends and family aren't quite persuaded or willing to start the same diet as you. There is a large community of low-carb fans out there, old and young, willing to interact and inspire others.

Why not try utilizing the low-carb community to gain support and keep motivated? As the adage goes, there is strength in numbers.

Be Clear With Your Goals

Setting objectives is a crucial component of being successful. They assist you to be clear about why you are making changes and how you will attain your objective within a set amount of time.

For most, attaining a goal is addicting, since it rewards you with a fantastic feeling of success. Usually, after people have attained their objective, they continue to create other aims, assisting them to continually grow.

Think of your objectives as your destination, it's where you want to go within a certain time limit. It is frequently good to establish both short-term and long-term objectives.

For example, a short-term aim would be to enhance your physical activity by walking for 30 minutes each day.

A longer-term objective could be to have your HbA1c under 6% (42mmol/mol).

Track Your Progress

Tracking your progress during your transition to a low-carb diet is tremendously useful in your growth.

Not only does it assist to keep you motivated, but it is also beneficial when making objectives since it helps you to split big goals into smaller, more attainable ones.

In addition, monitoring progress might assist you to discover hurdles or failures in your trip, consequently allowing you to make required modifications.

For people living with diabetes, measuring your success may encompass so much more than merely concentrating on the scale.

Try measuring your blood sugar levels throughout the day more often and maintain a record of your HbA1c readings and blood pressure.

It is also beneficial to take weekly measures of other sections of your body, for example, your waist, hips, thighs, and arms.

Why not try maintaining a journal of how you feel along your trip, by jotting down your energy levels, and motivation levels and reporting on your progress?

It is generally beneficial to take regular progress shots or choose a pair of pants and write down how loose they feel regularly. This may be tremendously encouraging when they start to feel looser.

Share Your Journey with Friends and Family

Sometimes even our closest and dearest may be a huge source of sabotage in our diet objectives. They presumably don't even realize they are doing it.

They may nonetheless be our most trusted support network and can well aid you in accomplishing your objectives

Talking to your friends and family and letting them know you are going low carb can assist them to feel engaged in your journey and avoid them from placing temptation in your way.

This is particularly true if your motives are to better the management of your diabetes.

Check with Your Doctor

Consult with your doctor if you are taking medication. As with any modifications to your diet, there may be consequences to your medication requirements.

Keep It Simple

We want your time on the Low Carb Program to be as stress-free and joyful as possible. For this reason, we don't want you to become bogged down with calculating carbohydrates or calories.

Simply aim to lower your carb intake by eliminating starchy sources from your diet and raising your fat content. The rest will fall into place.

Meal Prep & Low Carb Snack Supply

For anybody who has dieted previously, you may already be aware of the advantages of planning out your meals and preparing them in bulk.

For those who are new to this, the benefits of meal preparation are that it not only helps to save you time and money but more significantly it helps to guarantee you stick to your objectives.

It takes away the temptation to graze or not bother preparing anything following your objectives since your meals and snacks are already prepared and ready to go.

If you are stumped for ideas consider utilizing the meal planning and snack ideas featured in this book.

Remove Temptation

So, all of your meals are packed for the next few days and you have a range of healthy snacks available for when you are feeling peckish, but there is still that loaf of bread and a multipack of chips screaming out from the cabinets to be eaten.

To prevent temptation such as this, we strongly advocate giving it away and eliminating it from your surroundings.

If you live with folks who aren't pursuing a low-carb diet, and this isn't an option for you, consider asking them to be discreet and supportive of your objectives.

Learn How to Eat Out

Life is for living and although you may be ready to start a new lifestyle that could limit you from eating particular foods, we still want you to have fun.

That's why we want you to learn how to eat out, so you can still enjoy social situations, without harming your progress on the Low Carb Program.

It's easier than you would imagine. Our top advice is to check the menu prior if possible. Always go for a source of protein, such as meat or fish, and switch any carbohydrate-heavy sides such as fries, for a side of fibrous greens or garden salad.

We also recommend requesting for some additional sources of fat on your meal, such as butter, olive oil, cheese, or low-carb spices such as mayonnaise and hollandaise.

It's not that hard to dine out on a low-carb diet, and the more you do it the more confident you'll get.

The low-carb community is a terrific place to seek support if you are ever stuck for ideas.

Include a Low Carb Treat

As we have previously discussed, we want you to still be able to enjoy life and have fun after reading and practicing everything in this book.

That's why we want you to ensure you incorporate a little bit of something delectable in your diet, whether that be a couple of pieces of plain dark chocolate or a gin and slimline tonic.

There are a lot of low-carb snacks to be enjoyed and I have supplied some ideas under the section 'low carb snacks'.

This is also a possibility for those of you who enjoy getting into the kitchen to experiment with some low-carb baking if that's your idea of a treat.

CHAPTER 2

Staples of a Low Sodium Low Carb Diet

2.1 Low-Sodium Foods to Include in Your Diet

Sodium is required for life, though not in the huge amounts most of us ingest.

If we never added salt to whatever we ate or cooked, we would still receive more than enough from the prepared and packaged items in our diet.

In addition to its excellent features, salt causes high blood pressure and weight growth.

These result in a variety of fatal diseases, such as the big three... diabetes, cancer, and cardiovascular diseases.

You can see it's crucial to regulate the salt in your diet, but it's also simple to handle, whether you're in the store, the restaurant, or cooking in your own house.

Prepared Food Labels And Sodium: First, shopping to minimize salt is an issue of balance. You can't rule salt out of your life. The idea is to purchase fewer products with high salt levels.

So, it's vital to know what quantity is in there. That's where the food nutrition labels are useful. They tell you how much salt is in each single serving. For prepared meals, (soups, frozen dinners, entrée, chili, etc.)

I utilize the "500 rule." If it's about 500mg per serving, it's OK. You'll encounter dishes with salt as high as 2,000 mg per serving.

That's nearly as much salt as you should consume in an entire day, crammed into one small portion. You just can't go wrong with the fresh fruits and veggies department.

Though celery is high in sodium, it would require a lot of celery to cause a problem.

Canned veggies do contain extra sodium...some have a lot. Sauces and sauces frequently carry a boatload of salt. Once we create a habit of studying the labels, it's easier to make the right decisions in the supermarket to lower the sodium we eat. The most challenging spot is the restaurant.

Eating Out With Less Salt: As we discovered at the store, salt is in most of the foods we purchase.

So, if they didn't add salt to their recipes, restaurant food would already contain plenty...but they do add salt...usually lots of it.

I used to work as a cook...trust me about the salt. That's what made restaurant cuisine so good and what keeps us going back for another meal.

If we're controlling our salt, we should dine out less frequently and follow three easy principles when we do:

1. Ask for dressings and sauces on the side. Dressings and sauces are added to dishes for taste. For instance, if you order them on the side, you may add as much or as little as you like, obtaining the taste, but limiting the quantity of salt.

2. Plan for a doggie bag. I know! Our parents taught us to clear our dishes so we could eat dessert.

You're in command, now. Most restaurants serve you at least two times as much food as you need in one sitting.

To reduce the salt, split the portions in half and take ½ home for a snack.

3. Shake the shaker habit. We went out with another couple for hamburgers one day. We were brought one enormous serving of fries.

I was appalled when, without tasting them, he put salt all over the fries. The salt shaker is a negative habit many individuals have.

Restaurant fries already have salt on them. The Catsup you dip them in contains loads of salt.

The spicy sauce you put on them contains salt. You don't need the salt shaker at the restaurant.

Cooking Low Sodium Foods: Since we discovered at the shop how much salt is already in our food, adding extra when cooking simply doesn't make sense.

At home, it's more logical for each to use a salt shaker if they desire to enhance the taste. Marsha and I are unaware that where our salt shaker is. Several pastry recipes demand salt for the recipe to work.

This isn't the case with any meats, poultry, fish, or vegetable. Homemade soups employ a soup foundation (or cube) filled with salt.

Canned beans and tomatoes provide enough salt to flavor the complete serving of spaghetti or chili. We can generally simply line out the salt in our list of ingredients and still have enough taste.

With vegetables, try fresh ground pepper or crushed garlic (not garlic salt) instead of salt.

Cooking at home is where you have the greatest control over the salt in your diet.

You can decrease the salt in your meals whether you're shopping, dining out, or cooking at home.

We start by recognizing salt is in everything and restricting those items that are rich in salt.

Before long, our tastes change and we begin liking the natural flavor of the foods rather than the salt we used to add to them.

It's feasible to lower our typical salt consumption in half without losing anything in taste. Yes, you can!

2.2 Low-Carb Foods to Include in Your Diet

Many individuals don't begin a low-carb diet or don't remain with it, simply because they can't find appealing selections that are also low in carbs.

Many foods can be used for meals, in recipes, or for snacks, when you're trying to maintain a diet that is low in carbs.

Consuming a range of foods that are naturally low in carbs can help you to consume a nutritious diet that's pleasant and also excellent for you.

Everyone is unique, and the same meals won't work for everyone, but some foods are quite popular on low-carb diets, and you can adapt your recipes to fit your preferences.

Fish is a common mainstay on low-carb diets. But you do not need to limit yourself to merely the well-known types. There are many fantastic low-carbohydrate meals, and fresh fish is a healthy element of your low-carb diet that you should consume at least several times a week.

The finest fish for your diet could be orange roughy, Alaskan halibut, trout, wild-caught salmon, sea bass, cod, and mackerel.

Shellfish are healthful low-carb alternatives that are full of flavor, too.

They include scallops, crab, shrimp, oysters, clams, and lobster.

Eggs and egg whites may be included as breakfast necessities or as components in other meals. Free-range eggs are generally recommended in low-carb diets.

You're not restricted to chicken eggs, either. You could choose to try quail or duck eggs, to keep your diet lively and diverse from one day to the next.

Red meat is an essential mainstay in low carbohydrate diets since it helps you to acquire adequate protein for a balanced diet. Lamb is a wonderful option, as is venison or deer meat.

Cattle that have been grass-fed will be a favorable option, as would buffalo or bison meat, as long as the animals weren't treated with antibiotics or growth hormones.

Poultry may be added in many low-carbohydrate dishes, to make them palatable.

Consume only chicken that was never treated with antibiotics or hormones. Some of the most common poultry selections include chicken, duck, goose, and turkey.

Wild bird meat is also on the list of wonderful low-carb ingredients that give superb low-carbohydrate dish foundations, so include pheasant, wild turkey, and quail to your list.

You should incorporate vegetables and fruits in any diet, too, so that you receive the advantages of their various vitamins and minerals.

Vegetables that are not starchy are the greatest for your diet, including collard greens and spinach.

Good-tasting veggies to utilize for meals and healthful snacks or salads include Romaine lettuce, cauliflower, asparagus, cucumbers, mushrooms, turnip greens, and celery.

You may also add cabbage, zucchini, cilantro, and mustard greens. Vegetable leaves and stems might allow you to produce nutritious salads that are low in carbs.

Fresh fruits are fantastic options, as elements of meals or as snacks. Include fresh strawberries, raspberries, and blueberries, and eliminate any carb count from your allowance for each day.

These include sugar and carbs, so they ought to be enjoyed sparingly.

Oils contribute omega fatty acids to your diet, so utilize them as desired in your recipes. Some of the finest options are extra virgin olive oil, flaxseed, and canola oils.

By incorporating all these various fantastic low-carb meals, you may add good flavor to your low-carb, heart-healthy diet.

2.3 Foods to Avoid

Low-sodium and low-carb diets are popular among individuals trying to maintain a healthy lifestyle.

But not all low-sodium and low-carb foods are created equal. Certain foods that are low in sodium and carbohydrates can still be unhealthy and must be avoided for optimal health and wellness.

Highly processed meals such as low-sodium chips, crackers, and snack foods are frequently filled with harmful fats, salt, and carbs.

These processed meals frequently have very little nutritional value and may be hazardous to your health if taken in big numbers.

Even if the food item is branded as "low-sodium" or "low-carb," be careful to examine the nutrition information label to be sure these claims are real.

Canned meals are typically rich in salt, even if it is advertised as low-sodium.

Canned vegetables, soups, beans, and other products are commonly packaged in a salty brine solution and may contain up to 600mg of sodium per serving.

Many canned fruits also contain added sugar, which can increase the carbohydrate content of a meal.

Processed meats, such as hot dogs, bacon, and lunch meats, are generally rich in salt, fat, and carbs.

These sorts of meats are frequently cured with salt and are sometimes mixed with harmful fats and additives.

Processed meats may also include nitrates, which have been related to several health issues.

Fried meals, such as French fries, onion rings, and chicken nuggets, are generally heavy in salt and carbs.

These meals are frequently cooked in harmful fats, such as trans fats, which are known to raise the risk of heart disease.

Many condiments and sauces, such as ketchup and salad dressings, are also high in sodium and carbohydrates. These condiments are frequently filled with sugar and artificial flavorings and should be avoided if possible.

Frozen meals are frequently minimal in salt and carbs, but may still be harmful.

These sorts of meals are frequently heavy in fat and calories and might include harmful substances such as preservatives and artificial flavorings.

Candy and other sweets are generally heavy in carbs and might contain a surprising amount of salt.

Many candies and sweets contain unhealthy fats, such as trans fats, and should be avoided.

Alcoholic drinks may also be heavy in carbs and salt.

Beer and wine are often heavy in carbs, and many mixed beverages have added sugar.

Soda is one of the biggest offenders when it comes to harmful, high-sodium, and high-carbohydrate diets.

Soda is laden with added sugar and may contain up to 500mg of salt per drink.

The easiest approach to keeping healthy is to avoid these harmful, high-sodium, and high-carbohydrate meals.

Instead, choose fresh, whole, unprocessed meals such as fruits and vegetables, lean meats, and whole grains.

Eating a healthy, balanced diet is the greatest approach to guarantee a lifetime of excellent health.

Low-sodium and low-carb items to avoid include processed foods, canned foods, processed meats, fried meals, condiments, sauces, frozen dinners, candies, sweets, alcoholic drinks, and soda.

Eating a healthy, balanced diet rich in fresh, unprocessed foods is the greatest approach to guarantee a lifetime of excellent health.

CHAPTER 3

Low Sodium Low Carb Breakfast Recipes

3.1 Egg Muffins

Ingredients:

- 2 tablespoons olive oil

- 1/2 cup diced red bell pepper

- 1/2 cup diced onion

- 2 cups diced cooked ham - 12 eggs

- 1/4 cup milk

- 1/4 teaspoon salt

- 1/4 teaspoon pepper

- 1/2 cup shredded cheddar cheese

Instructions:

1. Preheat oven to 350 degrees.

2. Grease a muffin tray with non-stick cooking spray.

3. Warm the olive oil in a big pan over medium heat.

4. Add the bell pepper and onion and simmer for 5 minutes, stirring periodically, until veggies are softened.

5. Add the diced ham and simmer for a further 5 minutes.

6. Remove skillet from heat and put aside to cool.

7. In a large bowl, mix the eggs, milk, salt, and pepper.

8. Add the cooled veggies and ham and mix to incorporate.

9. Split the egg blend equally between the 12 muffin cups.

10. Spread the grated cheese over the lid of each muffin.

11. Bake in preheated oven for 15-20 minutes, 12. Allow to cool before serving.

Prep Time: 15 minutes

Cook Time: 20 minutes

Total Time: 35 minutes

Nutritional information:

Nutrients	Amount per serving
Calories	130-150 kcal
Fat	10-12g
Protein	9g
Carbohydrates	1-2g
Fiber	1-2g
Cholesterol	200-250g
Sodium	150-200g
Vitamins	1mcg (5% DV)

3.2 Overnight Oats:

#1 Peanut Butter Banana Overnight Oats

Ingredients:

-1/4 cup of rolled oats

-1/4 cup of milk of your choice

-1 spoonful of peanut butter

-1/2 mashed banana

-A pinch of cinnamon -A fraction of salt

Instructions:

1. In a medium-sized dish, mix the rolled oats, milk, peanut butter, mashed banana, cinnamon, and salt.

2. Stir until all the ingredients are properly incorporated.

3. Place the mixture into a mason jar or other airtight container and chill overnight.

4. In the morning, take the oats from the refrigerator and give them a toss before consuming them.

Prep Time: 5 minutes

Refrigeration Time: 8-12 hours

Total Time: 8-12 hours, 5 minutes

Nutritional information:

Nutrients	Amount per serving
Calories	290
Fat	10g
Protein	12g
Potassium	200mg
Fiber	7g
Calcium	30mg
Magnesium	24mg

#2 Coconut Almond Chia Overnight Oats

Ingredients:

-1/4 cup of rolled oats

-1/4 cup of coconut milk

-1 tablespoon of chia seeds

-1 tablespoon of almond butter

-1 tablespoon of shredded coconut

-A sprinkling of cinnamon

-A pinch of salt

Instructions:

1. In a medium-sized bowl, mix the rolled oats, coconut milk, chia seeds, almond butter, shredded coconut, cinnamon, and salt.

2. Stir until all the ingredients are properly incorporated.

3. Place the mixture into a mason jar or other airtight container and chill overnight.

4. In the morning, take the oats from the refrigerator and give them a toss before consuming them.

Prep Time: 5 minutes

Refrigeration Time: 8-12 hours

Total Time: 8-12 hours, 5 minutes

Nutritional information:

Nutrients	Amount per serving
Calories	371 kcal
Protein	8.1g
Vitamin K	2 %
Fiber	8.1g
Calcium	237mg
Magnesium	54mg

3.3 Avocado Toast

Avocado Toast with Tomato & Feta

Ingredients:

-1 ripe avocado

-1/4 cup chopped tomatoes

-1/4 cup crumbled feta cheese

-1 teaspoon olive oil

-1/4 teaspoon garlic powder

-2 pieces of toast

Instructions:

1. Halve the avocado and remove the pit. Scoop out the meat and mash it in a basin with a fork.

2. Add the chopped tomatoes, feta cheese, olive oil, and garlic powder to the mashed avocado and stir until everything is mixed.

3. Toast the pieces of bread.

4. Spread the avocado mixture onto the bread.

5. Serve and enjoy!

Prep Time: 10 minutes

Cook Time: 5 minutes

Total Time: 15 minutes

Nutritional information: *(DV = Daily Value)

Nutrients	Amount per serving
Calories	300-350 kcal
Fat	15-20g
Protein	10g
Vitamin A	10-15 %
Fiber	8g
Calcium	10 % DV
Potassium	15-20 DV

3.4 Zucchini Pancakes

Ingredients:

2 cups grated zucchini

1 cup flour

1/2 cup milk

2 eggs

1 teaspoon baking powder

1/2 teaspoon salt

1/4 teaspoon garlic powder

1/4 teaspoon onion powder

1/4 cup grated Parmesan cheese

3 tablespoons olive oil

Instructions:

1. In a medium bowl, mix the flour, baking powder, salt, garlic powder, and onion powder.

2. In a separate dish, mix the eggs, milk, and oil.

3. Add the wet ingredients to the dry ingredients, stirring until just blended.

4. Stir in the shredded zucchini and Parmesan cheese.

5. Heat a big skillet over medium heat and grease with a tiny quantity of oil.

6. Drop a heaping spoonful of the batter onto the pan and spread it into a pancake shape.

7. Cook for 2-3 minutes till golden brown, then turn and cook the opposite side for 2-3 minutes.

8. Move to a plate and replicate with the remaining batter.

Prep Time: 10 minutes

Cook Time: 10 minutes

Total Time: 20 minutes

Nutritional information: *(DV = Daily Value)

Nutrients	Amount per serving
Calories	150 kcal
Fat	7-10g
Protein	7-10g
Vitamin A	8-10 % DV
Vitamin C	10-15 % DV
Fiber	2-4g
Calcium	4-6 % DV
Potassium	8-10 % DV
Iron	8-10 %

3.5 Smoothies

Banana Berry Smoothie

Ingredients:

-1 ripe banana

-1 cup frozen mixed berries

-1 cup almond milk

-1 tbsp honey -1 teaspoon ground flaxseed

Instructions:

1. Place the banana, berries, almond milk, honey, and flaxseed in a blender.

2. Blend until smooth.

3. Pour into glasses and enjoy!

Prep Time: 5 minutes

Nutritional Value: *(DV = Daily Value)

Nutrients	Amount per serving
Calories	150-250 kcal
Fat	1-3g
Protein	3-5g
Vitamin C	30-50 % DV
Fiber	3-6g
Potassium	10-15 % DV

Sugars	15-25g

Mango Coconut Smoothie

Ingredients:

-1 ripe mango, peeled, pitted and chopped

-1 cup coconut milk

-1/4 cup plain Greek yogurt

-1 tbsp honey -1 teaspoon chia seeds

Instructions:

1. Place the mango, coconut milk, yogurt, honey, and chia seeds in a blender.

2. Blend until smooth.

3. Pour into glasses and enjoy!

Prep Time: 5 minutes

Nutritional information: *(DV = Daily Value)

Nutrients	Amount per serving
Calories	181-220 kcal
Saturated fats	1.2g
Sugars	22-28g
Protein	8.1g
Vitamin C	100 % DV
Fiber	3g
Potassium	237mg
Magnesium	10 % DV
Manganese	20 % DV

Strawberry Avocado Smoothie

Ingredients:

-1 cup frozen strawberries

-1 medium avocado, peeled and chopped

-1 cup almond milk

-1 tablespoon honey

-1 teaspoon ground flaxseed

Instructions:

1. Place the strawberries, avocado, almond milk, honey, and flaxseed in a blender.

2. Blend until smooth.

3. Pour into glasses and enjoy!

Prep Time: 5 minutes

Nutritional information: *(DV = Daily Value)

Nutrients	Amount per serving
Calories	197-238 kcal
Saturated fats	3g
Sugars	15g
Protein	8.1g
Vitamin C	100 % DV
Fiber	7g
Potassium	10 % DV
Folate	20 % DV

CHAPTER 4

Low Sodium Low Carb Lunch Recipes

4.1 Salmon Cakes

Ingredients:

-1 pound cooked salmon, flaked

-2 big eggs

-1/2 cup finely chopped onion

-1/2 cup Italian-style breadcrumbs

-2 tablespoons mayonnaise

-1 tbsp Dijon mustard

-1 tablespoon freshly squeezed lemon juice

-1 teaspoon dried dill

-1/4 teaspoon garlic powder

-1/4 teaspoon salt

-1/4 teaspoon freshly ground black pepper

-2 tablespoons olive oil

Instructions:

1. In a medium bowl, mix the flakes salmon, eggs, onion, breadcrumbs, mayonnaise, mustard, lemon juice, dill, garlic powder, salt, and pepper. Mix until all components are fully combined.

2. Form the mixture into 8 patties.

3. In a large pan over medium heat, heat the olive oil.

4. Add the salmon cakes to the pan and cook for approximately 5 minutes per side, or until light brown and cooked through.

5. Serve warm.

Prep Time: 20 minutes

Cook Time: 10 minutes

Total Time: 30 minutes

Nutritional information: (*DV = Daily Value)

Nutrients	Amount per serving
Calories	180 kcal
Total fat	10g
Cholesterol	95mg
Protein	16g
Sodium	340mg
Vitamin D	1.5mcg (8%DV)
Potassium	220mg (5% DV)
Calcium	60mg (6% DV)

4.2 Vegetable Wraps

Vegetable Wrap Recipe

Ingredients:

- 4 large flour tortillas

- ½ cup cooked black beans

- ½ cup cooked corn

- ½ cup cooked quinoa

- ½ red bell pepper, chopped

- ½ green bell pepper, diced

- ½ cup diced red onion

- ½ cup shredded cheese

- ½ cup of your favorite salsa

- 2 tablespoons olive oil

- Salt and pepper, to taste

Instructions:

1. Preheat oven to 350 degrees F.

2. In a medium bowl, mix black beans, corn, quinoa, bell peppers, red onion, cheese, and salsa. Season to taste with salt and pepper.

3. Place the tortillas on a baking sheet. Brush each one gently with olive oil.

4. Divide the vegetable mixture between the four tortillas, spreading it equally over the top.

5. Bake for 15 minutes, or until the tortillas are golden brown and the cheese has melted.

6. Serve warm.

Prep Time: 10 minutes

Cook Time: 15 minutes

Total Time: 25 minutes

Nutritional information: (*DV = Daily Value)

Nutrients	Amount per serving
Calories	350 kcal
Total fat	15g
Total carb	45mg
Protein	10g
Sodium	680mg
Fiber	10g
Potassium	600mg (15% DV)
Calcium	120mg (10% DV)

4.3 Quinoa Bowls

Quinoa & Veggie Bowl

Ingredients:

-1 cup Quinoa

-1 cup mixed veggies (such as broccoli, carrots, peppers, and peas)

- 2 tablespoons olive oil

- 1 teaspoon garlic powder

- 1 teaspoon onion powder

- Salt and pepper to taste

Instructions:

1. Preheat oven to 400°F.

2. Cook the quinoa according to the package directions and put it aside.

3. Place the veggies in a large bowl and add olive oil, garlic powder, onion powder, salt, and pepper. Toss to coat.

4. Spread the veggies on a baking sheet and bake for 20 minutes.

5. When the veggies have done cooking, add them to the cooked quinoa and toss to blend.

6. Serve warm.

Prep Time: 10 minutes

Cook Time: 20 minutes

Total Time: 30 minutes

Nutritional information: (*DV = Daily Value)

Nutrients	Amount per serving
Calories	400 kcal
Total fat	16g
Total carb	54mg
Protein	11g
Sodium	180mg

Iron	4mg (22% DV)
Potassium	780mg (17% DV)
Calcium	80mg (6% DV)

Quinoa & Avocado Bowl

Ingredients:

- 1 cup quinoa

- 1 avocado, chopped

- ½ cup diced tomatoes

- ½ cup chopped bell pepper

- 2 tablespoons olive oil

- 1 teaspoon cumin

- Juice of 1 lime

- Salt and pepper to taste directions:

Instructions:

1. Cook the quinoa according to package directions and put it aside.

2. Place the avocado, tomatoes, and bell pepper in a large bowl and add olive oil, cumin, lime juice, salt, and pepper. Toss to coat.

3. Add the veggies to the cooked quinoa and toss to incorporate.

4. Serve warm.

Prep Time: 10 minutes

Cook Time: 15 minutes

Nutritional information: (*DV = Daily Value)

Nutrients	Amount per serving
Calories	380 kcal
Total fat	20g
Total carb	43mg

Protein	10g
Sodium	150mg
Fiber	12g
Potassium	680mg (15% DV)
Calcium	60mg (4% DV)

4.4 Zucchini Noodles

Avocado Pesto Zucchini Noodles

Ingredients:

-3 zucchini, spiralized

-1/4 cup olive oil

-2 cloves garlic, minced

-1/2 cup fresh basil leaves

-2 avocados, peeled and pitted

-1/4 cup walnuts

-1/4 cup Parmesan cheese

-1/4 teaspoon salt

-1/4 teaspoon black pepper

Instructions:

1. In a big pan, heat the olive fat over medium heat.

2. Add the garlic and simmer for 1 minute, stirring regularly.

3. Add the zucchini noodles and simmer for 5 minutes, stirring regularly.

4. In a blender or food processor, mix the basil, avocados, walnuts, Parmesan cheese, salt, and pepper. Blend until smooth.

5. Pour the pesto over the zucchini noodles and mix to incorporate.

6. Cook for a further 2 minutes, stirring periodically.

7. Serve and enjoy!

Prep Time: 15 minutes

Cook Time: 7 minutes

Total Time: 22 minutes

Nutritional information: (*DV = Daily Value)

Nutrients	Amount per serving
Calories	300 kcal
Total fat	25g
Cholesterol	3mg
Total carb	16mg
Protein	8g
Sodium	90mg
Fiber	7g
Potassium	720mg (15% DV)
Calcium	120mg (10% DV)

2. Zucchini Noodle Pad Thai

Ingredients:

-3 zucchini, spiralized

-2 tablespoons olive oil

-2 cloves garlic, minced

-1/2 red bell pepper, diced

-1/2 cup snow peas

-1/4 cup soy sauce

-1 tbsp honey

-1 teaspoon sriracha

-1/4 cup peanuts, chopped

-2 tablespoons fresh cilantro chopped

Instructions:

1. In a big pan, heat the olive fat over medium heat.

2. Add the garlic and simmer for 1 minute, stirring regularly.

3. Add the bell pepper and snow peas and simmer for 3 minutes, stirring regularly.

4. Add the zucchini noodles and simmer for 5 minutes, stirring regularly.

5. In a small bowl, stir together the soy sauce, honey, and sriracha.

6. Pour the sauce over the zucchini noodles and mix to incorporate.

7. Cook for a further 2 minutes, stirring occasionally.

8. Serve garnished with chopped peanuts and cilantro. Enjoy!

Prep Time: 15 minutes

Cook Time: 10 minutes

Total Time: 25 minutes

Nutritional information: (*DV = Daily Value)

Nutrients	Amount per serving
Calories	350 kcal
Total fat	20g
Cholesterol	95mg
Total carb	32mg
Protein	14g
Sodium	650mg
Fiber	6g
Potassium	620mg (15% DV)
Calcium	100mg (8% DV)

4.5 Broccoli Soup

Ingredients:

-4 cups of broccoli florets

-2 teaspoons of butter

-2 cloves of garlic, minced

-1 onion, diced

-2 tablespoons of all-purpose flour

-4 cups of chicken broth

-1/2 cup of heavy cream

-Salt and pepper to taste

Instructions:

1. In a big saucepan, melt the butter over medium heat.

2. Add the garlic and onion and sauté until the onions are mellow and aromatic, approximately 5 minutes.

3. Add the flour and mix to blend.

4. Gradually add the chicken broth, stirring frequently to prevent lumps.

5. Add the broccoli florets and bring to a boil. Decrease the heat and steam for 10 minutes, or until the broccoli is smooth.

6. Remove from the heat and use an immersion blender to mix the soup until smooth.

7. Stir in the heavy cream and season with salt and pepper to taste.

8. Serve warm.

Prep Time: 15 minutes

Cook Time: 20 minutes

Nutritional information: (*   DV = Daily Value)

Nutrients	Amount per serving
Calories	120 kcal
Total fat	6g
Cholesterol	15mg
Total carb	14mg

Protein	5g
Sodium	700mg
Fiber	4g
Potassium	550mg (10% DV)
Calcium	130mg (10% DV)

CHAPTER 5

Low Sodium Low Carb Dinner Recipes

5.1 Baked Tilapia

Recipe: Baked Tilapia with Fennel and Orange

Ingredients:

- 4 tilapia fillets

- 2 tablespoons olive oil

- 2 tablespoons freshly squeezed orange juice

- 1/4 teaspoon sea salt

- 1/4 teaspoon freshly ground black pepper

- 2 cloves garlic, minced

- 1 fennel bulb, thinly sliced

- 1/4 cup white wine

- 2 teaspoons chopped fresh parsley

Instructions:

1. Preheat the oven to 375°F.

2. In a shallow baking dish, mix the olive oil, orange juice, sea salt, black pepper, and garlic. Add the tilapia fillets and flip to coat.

3. Top the fish with the fennel pieces. Pour the white wine over the fish and fennel.

4. Bake for 20 minutes, or until the fish is cooked through.

5. Sprinkle with chopped parsley and serve.

Prep Time: 10 minutes

Cook Time: 20 minutes

Total Time: 30 minutes

Nutritional information: (*DV = Daily Value)

Nutrients	Amount per serving
Calories	220 kcal
Total fat	8g
Cholesterol	60mg
Total carb	10mg
Protein	28g
Vitamin D	10 % DV
Sodium	350mg
Fiber	3g
Potassium	15 % DV
Calcium	6 % DV

5.2 Chicken and Veggie Stir Fry

Ingredients:

- 2 teaspoons vegetable oil

- 2 boneless, skinless chicken breasts, diced

- 1 onion, diced

- 2 cloves garlic, minced

- 2 carrots, peeled and sliced

- 2 celery stalks, cut

- 1 red bell pepper, chopped

- 2 cups broccoli florets

- 2 teaspoons low-sodium soy sauce

- 2 tablespoons oyster sauce

- 1 teaspoon sesame oil

- 2 tablespoons water

- Salt and pepper, to taste

Instructions:

1. Heat the oil in a big pan over medium heat.

2. Add the chicken and fry until browned and cooked through, approximately 5 minutes.

3. Add the onion, garlic, carrots, celery, and bell pepper and simmer for 3 minutes.

4. Add the broccoli and cook for a further 2 minutes.

5. Add the soy sauce, oyster sauce, sesame oil, and water. Stir to mix.

6. Cook for a further 2 minutes.

7. Season to taste with salt and pepper.

8. Serve hot.

Prep Time: 15 minutes

Cook Time: 10 minutes

Total Time: 25 minutes

Nutritional information: (*DV = Daily Value)

Nutrients	Amount per serving
Calories	350 kcal
Total fat	12g
Cholesterol	75mg
Total carb	20mg

Protein	40g
Vitamin C	80 % DV
Sodium	700mg
Fiber	4g
Potassium	20 % DV
Calcium	4 % DV

5.3 Grilled Salmon

Grilled Salmon with Lemony Broccoli

Ingredients:

-2 salmon fillets

-2 tbsp olive oil

-2 cloves of garlic, minced

-Juice of 1 lemon

-1/2 tsp salt

-1/4 tsp black pepper

-1 head of broccoli, cut into florets

-1/2 tsp Italian seasoning

Instructions:

1. Preheat your grill to medium-high heat.

2. In a small bowl, mix the olive oil, garlic, lemon juice, salt, and pepper.

3. Place the salmon fillets on a platter and brush with the olive oil mixture.

4. Place the salmon on the grill and cook for 3-4 minutes on each side, or until the fish flakes easily with a fork.

5. In a large dish, mix the broccoli with the remaining marinade.

6. Place the broccoli on the grill and cook for 3-4 minutes, or until tender.

7. Sprinkle with Italian spice and serve over the cooked fish.

Prep Time: 10 minutes

Cook Time: 10 minutes

Total Time: 20 minutes

Nutritional information: (*DV = Daily Value)

Nutrients	Amount per serving
Calories	380 kcal
Total fat	22g
Cholesterol	90mg
Total carb	12mg
Protein	35g
Vitamin C	120 % DV
Sodium	450mg
Fiber	5g
Potassium	25 % DV
Calcium	10 % DV

5.4 Turkey Burgers

Ingredients:

-1 pound ground turkey

-1 egg

-1 teaspoon garlic powder

-1/4 cup breadcrumbs

-1/4 cup chopped onion

-1 teaspoon Worcestershire sauce

-Salt and pepper to taste

Instructions:

1. In a large bowl, mix the ground turkey, egg, garlic powder, breadcrumbs, onion, Worcestershire sauce, and salt and pepper.

2. Form the mixture into 4 patties.

3. Heat a pan over medium heat and add a couple of teaspoons of oil.

4. Place the turkey burgers in the pan and cook for 6-8 minutes on each side, or until the burgers are cooked through.

5. Serve the burgers with your chosen toppings.

Prep Time: 10 minutes

Cook Time: 15 minutes

Total Time: 25 minutes

Nutritional information: (*DV = Daily Value)

Nutrients	Amount per serving
Calories	250 kcal
Saturated Fat	3g
Cholesterol	80mg
Total carb	15mg
Protein	20g
Vitamin C	2 % DV
Sodium	350mg
Fiber	2g
Potassium	8 % DV
Calcium	6 % DV

5.5 Vegetable Curry

Ingredients:

- 2 teaspoons of vegetable oil

- 1 onion, diced

- 1 green bell pepper, chopped

- 2 cloves of garlic, minced

- 2 carrots, diced

- 2 potatoes, diced

- 1 teaspoon of curry powder

- 1 teaspoon of ground cumin

- 1 teaspoon of powdered coriander

- 1 teaspoon of turmeric

- 1 (14.5-ounce) can of chopped tomatoes

- 1 (14-ounce) can of coconut milk

- 2 cups of vegetable broth

- 1 cup of frozen peas - Salt and pepper to taste

Instructions:

1. Heat the oil in a big saucepan over medium heat.

2. Add the onion, bell pepper, garlic, carrots, and potatoes and simmer for 7-8 minutes, turning regularly, until the vegetables are softened.

3. Add the curry powder, cumin, coriander, and turmeric and simmer for 1 minute, stirring frequently.

4. Add the chopped tomatoes, coconut milk, and vegetable broth and bring to a boil.

5. Reduce the heat to low and simmer for 15-20 minutes, until the veggies are soft.

6. Add the frozen peas and simmer for a further 5 minutes.

7. Season to taste with salt and pepper.

8. Serve over cooked rice or quinoa.

Prep Time: 15 minutes

Cook Time: 30 minutes

Total Time: 45 minutes

Nutritional information: (*DV = Daily Value)

Nutrients	Amount per serving
Calories	250 kcal
Saturated Fat	5g
Sugars	10g
Total carb	35mg
Protein	8g
Vitamin C	60 % DV
Sodium	350mg
Fiber	8g
Potassium	25 % DV
Calcium	6 % DV

CHAPTER 6

Low Sodium, Low Carb Snacks

6.1 Low Sodium Snack Ideas

One of the simplest suggestions for adhering to a change of eating plan is arranging your meals beforehand.

If you can plan and prepare approximately a week ahead, it is much simpler to adhere to an eating schedule.

A lot of individuals adhere to this notion and perform extremely well for their three daily main meals, but when it comes to snacking spontaneity and temptation will frequently take over.

Snacks are where most accidental calories are ingested, it will start with a little of anything and conclude 150 or more calories later.

Here are a few grown-up snacks that perform excellently throughout the workplace, all-day athletic events or even to assist avoid the food court after a day of intensive shopping.

Apples are rich in fiber, low in calories, and simple to grab and go. Try sliced apple and peanut butter or hummus for extra protein.

Replace your salty, greasy crackers with a piece of apple, they taste fantastic with cheeses and spreads of all types.

Edamame is a delicious treat that can be purchased pre-cooked and pre-packaged. These delightful tiny legumes are just as simple to pick up and pop in your mouth as French fries and are so much healthy for you. Dip them in low-sodium soy sauce or rice wine vinegar.

A little cup of vegetable soup is highly satisfying and low in calories.

Homemade is better so that you can check all of the components however if we are talking about short snacks even a can of vegetarian soup would work but watch the salt.

Low-fat ricotta cheese is incredibly flexible, it provides taste and texture to many meals. Try spreading low-fat ricotta over a piece of whole wheat bread and sprinkle with cinnamon and a liberal spoonful of honey.

This simple and delightful meal includes calcium, fiber, and antioxidants and may quiet a crazy sweet craving.

We all know that lean protein is vital for weight reduction. Hard-boiled egg whites are a filling alternative and there are so many possibilities you will never grow tired of this delight.

Chop up the egg whites into an egg salad, season with your favorite herbs like chives, lemon thyme, or cilantro, and wrap it up in a lettuce leaf.

Make a fast & low-fat tuna salad with chopped red bell peppers and fill cooked egg whites, deviled egg style.

Greek-style yogurt is fantastic with nothing more than mixed fruit and a spoon but it is also a great basis for dipping sauces.

Get your carrot sticks, cut bell peppers, and celery or mixed vegetables of choice ready to dip into a delicious blend of yogurt, chopped basil & garlic.

This fake pesto dip will fill your tummy in the middle of the day and suppress your desire for salty food.

Make a salad kabob - spice up the commonplace by making it appear distinctive.

Substitute cucumber, one ounce total of fresh mozzarella cheese, cherry tomato, and basil on skewers or toothpicks. Dip in balsamic vinaigrette.

Try the same thing with fruit, pineapple grapes, and mandarin oranges all make fantastic fruit kabobs. Chill and pour a little lemon over them for a delicious summer treat

Next time you are at the grocery store, load up on healthful products that fit in your hand.

Almonds, carrot sticks, kiwi, peaches, baked banana chips, dried fruit and nut-based trail mix, and low-fat cheeses all make for wonderful snacks that you won't regret later.

6.2 Low-Carb Snack Ideas

Incorporating low-carb snacks in meals is quite significant as they keep you full and assist you to function better without putting on weight to your body.

Here are several suggestions that one might have to modify their lifestyle into a healthy one.

The type of weight reduction one achieves by combining low-carb snacks is excellent.

Living has generally gotten so hectic that we scarcely have time to contemplate what we are consuming. In such a condition, frequently we start snacking while sitting at home or working at the office which leads to weight gain and health troubles too.

Many times, we also skip a meal, which carries an even worse effect on our health.

Here comes into play low-carb snacks which can be readily added to our healthy diet food and may assist us in losing weight along with eating a healthy and balanced diet.

One needs to know that the foods that come out of vending machines have the worst influence on our health.

Candies, pretzels, and chips need to be replaced with low-calorie snacks that are genuinely good diet food and provide an equal percentage of all vital components.

Healthy Diet Meal Menu Ideas

We tend to consume the wrong foods when working. So the best thing to do is to carry along some low-calorie snacks. One may simply bring nuts and fruits to the workplace.

Even youngsters may bring them to school and when traveling eating good diet food would be any day preferable.

Start substituting the lunch with your youngster with more fruits and veggies.

Children should be provided more fresh veggies along with low-fat milk, cottage cheese, yogurt, cheese, and nuts as a part of their healthy food menu.

One may carry all these items with oneself to the office also to nibble in between. Here are some additional options that you might include as a diet snack.

Go for nuts that are high in proteins. Use nuts in puddings, cereal and even you may have peanut butter instead of conventional butter.

Indeed nothing can beat fruits and veggies as diet snacks. Include apples, berries, grapes, pomegranates, and oranges. Make vegetable dips such as spinach dip, or hummus.

Eat salads and soups as low-carb snacks during lunch. Ensure that your meal is light and you may have dairy products for dinner.

Drink sufficient water and avoid alcohol, energy drinks, and juices.

Artificial food is never a low-carb snack as many people imagine. Avoid artificial sweeteners.

Even if they are not a component of low-carb snacks.

CHAPTER 7

Low Sodium Low Carb Desserts

7.1 No-Bake Cheesecake

Ingredients:

- 8 ounces of reduced
-fat cream cheese

- 2 tablespoons sugar
-free sweetener

- 1 teaspoon vanilla extract

- 2 tablespoons heavy cream

- 1/4 cup fresh lemon juice

- 1/2 cup plain Greek yogurt

- 1/4 cup sugar-free graham cracker crumbs

Instructions:

1. In a large bowl, blend cream cheese, sugar-free sweetener, and vanilla essence. Batter with an electric mixer until fully blended.

2. Add in the heavy cream and lemon juice, and beat until creamy and smooth.

3. Add in the Greek yogurt and whisk until just blended.

4. Line an 8-inch round baking dish with parchment paper.

5. Spread the cream cheese mixture into the prepared dish.

6. Sprinkle the graham cracker crumbs over the top.

7. Place the pan in the refrigerator for at least 2 hours before serving.

Prep Time: 10 minutes

Chill Time: 2 hours

Total Time: 2 hours 10 minutes

Nutritional information: (*DV = Daily Value)

Nutrients	Amount per serving
Calories	350 kcal
Saturated Fat	15g
Cholesterol	80mg
Total carb	28mg
Protein	5g
Vitamin D	10 % DV
Sodium	250mg
Fiber	1g
Potassium	2 % DV
Calcium	10 % DV

7.2 Chocolate Avocado Mousse

Ingredients:

- 2 ripe avocados

- ¼ cup unsweetened cocoa powder

- 1 teaspoon pure vanilla extract

- Pinch of sea salt

- 2-4 tablespoons sweetener of your choice (honey, maple syrup, stevia, etc.)

Instructions:

1. Put all components in a blender or food processor.

2. Blend until smooth.

3. Taste and adjust sweetness as desired.

4. Serve cold.

Prep time: 10 minutes

Nutritional information: (*DV = Daily Value)

Nutrients	Amount per serving
Calories	200 kcal
Saturated Fat	3g
Total carb	20mg
Protein	4g
Vitamin C	8 % DV

Sodium	10mg
Fiber	8g
Potassium	15 % DV
Calcium	2 % DV

7.3 Coconut Flour Cupcakes

Ingredients:

- 1/4 cup coconut flour

- 1/4 teaspoon baking powder

- 2 eggs

- 1/4 cup almond milk

- 4 tablespoons melted coconut oil

- 2 teaspoons honey

- 1 teaspoon vanilla extract

- 1/4 teaspoon powdered cinnamon

Instructions:

1. Preheat oven to 350 degrees F. Grease a 12-cup muffin tray with nonstick cooking spray.

2. In a small bowl, mix the coconut flour, baking powder, and cinnamon.

3. In a bigger dish, mix the eggs, almond milk, coconut oil, honey, and vanilla extract.

4. Slowly incorporate the dry components into the wet ingredients, stirring until just blended.

5. Divide the batter equally among the muffin cups.

6. Bake for 18-20 minutes, or until a toothpick inserted into the middle of a cupcake comes out clean.

7. Let chill in the pan for 5 minutes before moving to a wire rack to cool fully.

Prep Time: 10 minutes

Bake Time: 20 minutes

Nutritional information: (*DV = Daily Value)

Nutrients	Amount per serving
Calories	180 kcal
Total Fat	10g
Cholesterol	60mg
Total carb	18mg
Protein	5g
Vitamin D	2 % DV
Sodium	180mg
Fiber	4g
Potassium	2 % DV
Calcium	4 % DV

7.4 Blueberry Crumble

Ingredients:

-1 cup fresh blueberries

-1/4 cup almond flour

-1/4 cup rolled oats

-1/4 teaspoon ground cinnamon

-1 teaspoon coconut oil

-1 tablespoon honey

Instructions:

1. Preheat oven to 350 degrees F.

2. Grease an 8x8 baking dish with coconut oil and leave aside.

3. In a medium bowl, mix blueberries, almond flour, rolled oats, and ground cinnamon and whisk to blend.

4. In a small dish, heat coconut oil and honey together and mix until blended.

5. Pour the coconut oil and honey mixture over the blueberry mixture, and stir until all ingredients are uniformly covered.

6. Pour the blueberry crumble mixture onto the oiled baking dish and smooth it out evenly.

7. Bake for 20 minutes, or until the top is brown and the blueberries are lapping.

8. Let cool before serving.

Prep Time: 10 minutes

Cook Time: 20 minutes

Nutritional information: (*DV = Daily Value)

Nutrients	Amount per serving
Calories	300 kcal
Total Fat	12g
Cholesterol	25mg
Total carb	45mg
Protein	4g
Vitamin C	15 % DV
Sodium	150mg
Fiber	5g
Potassium	6 % DV
Calcium	4 % DV

7.5 Almond Butter Cookies

Ingredients:

- 1/2 cup almond butter

- 1/4 cup honey

- 1/4 teaspoon baking soda

- 1/4 teaspoon ground cinnamon

- 1/4 teaspoon ground nutmeg

- 1/4 teaspoon ground ginger

- 1 egg

- 1/4 cup finely chopped almonds

Instructions:

1. Preheat oven to 350°F.

2. In a larger bowl, whisk together almond butter, honey, baking soda, cinnamon, nutmeg, and ginger.

3. Beat in egg until nicely mixed.

4. Stir in chopped almonds.

5. Drop cookie dough by tablespoon onto the prepared baking sheet.

6. Bake for 8-10 minutes or until golden brown.

7. Cool biscuits on a baking sheet for 1 minute before moving them to a wire rack to cool fully.

Prep Time: 10 minutes

Cook Time: 8-10 minutes

Servings: 12 cookies

Nutritional information: (*DV = Daily Value)

Nutrients	Amount per serving
Calories	120 kcal
Total Fat	9g
Cholesterol	10mg
Total carb	8mg
Protein	3g

Sodium	70mg
Fiber	1g
Potassium	2 % DV
Iron	4 % DV

CHAPTER 8

Low Sodium Low Carb Condiments and Sauces

8.1 Greek Yogurt

Greek Yogurt Tzatziki Sauce

Ingredients:

1 cup Greek Yogurt

-¼ cup cucumber, finely chopped

1 tablespoon fresh mint, finely chopped

-1 tablespoon fresh dill, finely chopped

-1 teaspoon garlic, minced

-2 tablespoons extra-virgin olive oil

-1 tablespoon fresh lemon juice

-Salt and pepper, to taste

Instructions:

1. In a medium bowl, mix yogurt, cucumber, mint, dill, garlic, olive oil, and lemon juice.

2. Mix until all components are uniformly distributed.

3. Season to taste with salt and pepper.

4. Cool for close to 1 hour before serving.

Prep Time: 10 minutes

Total Time: 1 hour 10 minutes

Nutritional information: (*DV = Daily Value)

Nutrients	Amount per serving
Calories	50 kcal
Saturated Fat	1.5g
Cholesterol	10mg
Total carb	3mg
Protein	3g
Vitamin C	2 % DV

Sodium	100mg
Potassium	2 % DV
Calcium	4 % DV

Greek Yogurt Ranch Dressing

Ingredients:

-1 cup Greek Yogurt

-¼ cup mayonnaise

-2 tablespoons parsley, minced

-2 tablespoons chives, minced

-2 teaspoons dill, minced

-1 teaspoon garlic powder

-1 teaspoon onion powder

-Salt and pepper, to taste

Instructions:

1. In a medium bowl, put yogurt, mayonnaise, parsley, chives, dill, garlic powder, and onion powder.

2. Mix until all ingredients are uniformly distributed.

3. Season to taste with salt and pepper.

4. Cool for close to 1 hour before serving.

Prep Time: 10 minutes

Total Time: 1 hour 10 minutes

Nutritional information: (*DV = Daily Value)

Nutrients	Amount per serving
Calories	70 kcal
Total Fat	5g
Cholesterol	10mg
Total carb	4mg
Protein	3g
Vitamin C	2 % DV
Sodium	150mg
Potassium	2 % DV

Calcium	2 % DV

8.2 Cashew Cheese Sauce

Ingredients:

-1 cup of raw cashews

-1/4 cup of almond milk

-1 tablespoon of nutritious yeast

-1 tablespoon of apple cider vinegar

-1/2 teaspoon of garlic powder

-1/2 teaspoon of onion powder

-1/2 teaspoon of sea salt

Instructions:

1. Soak the cashews in warm water for 1-2 hours.

2. Drain and rinse the cashews.

3. Place the cashews, almond milk, nutritional yeast, apple cider vinegar, garlic powder, onion powder, and sea salt in a high-speed blender.

4. Combine until the blend is smooth and creamy.

5. Transfer the sauce to a bowl and adjust the taste to your desire.

6. Serve over your favorite cuisine.

Prep Time: 10 minutes

Cook Time: 2 hours

Nutritional information: (*DV = Daily Value)

Nutrients	Amount per serving
Calories	120 kcal
Total Fat	8g
Total carb	8mg
Protein	5g
Sodium	180mg
Fiber	1g
Potassium	4 % DV

Calcium	2 % DV

Servings: 4-6 persons

8.3 Pesto

Ingredients:

- 2 cloves garlic, minced

- 2 cups fresh basil leaves, packed

- 2 tablespoons pine nuts

- 2 tablespoons freshly grated Parmesan cheese

- 2 tablespoons extra-virgin olive oil

- 2 teaspoons lemon juice

- Salt and pepper, to taste

Instructions:

1. In a food processor, blend garlic, basil, pine nuts, Parmesan cheese, olive oil, and lemon juice.

2. Blend until desired consistency is obtained.

3. Add salt and pepper to taste.

4. Serve with your favorite spaghetti, or as a dip for fresh veggies.

Prep Time: 10 minutes

Total Time: 10 minutes

Nutritional information: (*DV = Daily Value)

Nutrients	Amount per serving
Calories	150 kcal
Total Fat	15g
Total carb	3g
Protein	3g
Vitamin C	4 % DV
Sodium	200mg
Potassium	2 % DV
Calcium	4 % DV
Iron	6 % DV

8.4 Hummus with Roasted Red Pepper

Ingredients:

-1 can (15.5 oz) chickpeas, drained and rinsed

-1/4 cup tahini

-1/4 cup of lemon juice

-1/4 cup of olive oil

-1/4 cup of roasted red peppers

-1 garlic clove, minced

-1/4 teaspoon of salt

-1/4 teaspoon of ground cumin

Instructions:

1. In a food processor, blend chickpeas, tahini, lemon juice, olive oil, roasted red peppers, garlic, salt, and cumin.

2. Blend until smooth and creamy.

3. Serve with veggies, crackers, or pita chips. Enjoy!

Prep time: 10 minutes

Nutritional information: (*DV = Daily Value)

Nutrients	Amount per serving
Calories	100 kcal
Total Fat	6g
Total carb	10g
Protein	3g
Sodium	200mg
Fiber	3g
Potassium	4 % DV
Vitamin C	20 % DV

Note: This hummus is low in salt and low in carbs.

8.5 Guacamole

Ingredients:

- 2 ripe avocados

- 1/4 cup chopped onion

- 1/4 cup diced tomato

- 1/4 teaspoon garlic powder

- 1/4 teaspoon onion powder

- 1/4 teaspoon chili powder

- 1/4 teaspoon cumin

- 2 teaspoons lime juice

- Salt, to taste

Instructions:

1. Cut the avocados in half, remove the pit, and scoop the flesh into a medium mixing bowl.

2. Smash the avocados with a fork or potato masher until they reach a preferred texture.

3. Add the chopped onion, tomato, garlic powder, onion powder, chili powder, cumin, and lime juice. Combine until all the components are uniformly distributed.

4. Add salt to taste and combine one final time.

5. Serve and enjoy!

Prep Time: 10 minutes

Nutrition information: (*DV = Daily Value)

Nutrients	Amount per serving
Calories	120 kcal
Total Fat	10g
Total carb	8g
Protein	2g

Sodium	200mg
Fiber	5g
Potassium	8 % DV
Calcium	2 % DV

Nutritional data based on a 2,000-calorie diet.

CHAPTER 9

Low Sodium Low Carb Meal Planning

9.1 Meal Planning Tips

Nearly one in two persons in the United States have hypertension, the medical term for high blood pressure, and the incidence is somewhat greater when examining males alone.

If you are in this group or have other medical illnesses or concerns, there's a strong chance your doctor may prescribe following a low-sodium diet.

Although your body does require some salt — since it's a vital electrolyte involved in muscle contractions, conveying electrical impulses in the heart, and controlling fluid balance — the normal American diet is extraordinarily heavy in sodium.

Excess sodium leads to **high blood pressure** and may stress the heart over time.

The Dietary Guidelines for Americans suggest individuals restrict their daily sodium consumption to less than 2,300 mg per day, which is equivalent to one teaspoon of table salt, although 97% of guys aged 19-59 are above the recommended dose for their age.

In fact, according to an analysis, males aged 20-31 are consuming an average of 4,728 mg and while those 32-60 take 4,173 mg on average, which is over two times the recommended amount.

A low-sodium diet carefully reduces the amount of salt ingested each day and has been found to successfully lower blood pressure and enhance heart function.

It can be daunting to get started on a low-sodium diet, and it may feel like you have to give up some of your favorite foods, but the good news is that there are many delicious, nutritious foods you can still eat on a low-sodium diet and you're likely to feel so much better than any sacrifices will feel well worth it.

Keep reading for our comprehensive guide featuring all you need to know about a low-sodium diet.

What Is a Low-Sodium Diet?

Sodium, which is a different type of salt, is contained naturally in some foods like eggs and spinach, but the bulk of the sodium we eat is added to processed and prepared meals to increase the taste and shelf life.

Additional table salt enters the diet when individuals salt and season their meal before eating it.

A low-sodium diet generally restricts daily salt consumption to 1,500 mg, which is lower than the recommended daily limit of 2,300 mg and substantially lower than what the average American adult is ingesting.

Very low-sodium diets reduce sodium even more. High-sodium foods should be removed from the diet, and the focus should be on pure, natural, unprocessed foods with little to no table salt added.

When following a low-sodium diet, it's vitally crucial to check the nutrition label on any packaged item to measure the salt amount.

Look for items that have less than 140 mg of salt per serving. There are various labels placed on items to identify their salt level, including the following:

Salt/Sodium-Free: Must contain less than 5 mg of sodium per serving.

Very Low Sodium: Retain a utmost 35 mg of sodium per serving.

Low Sodium: Include an average of 149 mg of sodium per serving.

Reduced Sodium: The product includes at least 25% less sodium than the usual version although the particular sodium concentration may be anything.

Lightly Salty or Light In Sodium: The outcome includes at least 50% smaller sodium than the usual interpretation although the individual sodium concentration may be anything.

No-Salt-Added or Unsalted: No salt is added while producing the product although it may include natural sodium inherent in the components.

Benefits Of a Low-Sodium Diet

Because salt causes water retention, elevates blood pressure, and strains the heart and kidneys, adopting a low-sodium diet may result in the following benefits:

- Reduced blood pressure
- Weight loss
- Decreased risk of heart attack and stroke
- Improved kidney function, particularly in patients with renal disease
- Decreased edema and better circulation
- Improved diet quality

Foods to Avoid On a Low-Sodium Diet

People tend to assume that adding table salt to meals before eating it is the major perpetrator of excessive sodium levels, however, roughly 70% or more of the sodium most people are receiving comes from different salts included in prepared and processed foods.

The following foods are especially rich in sodium and should be avoided on a low-sodium diet:

Fast Food: French fries, onion rings, Burgers, tacos, chicken nuggets, pizza, fast food Chinese, etc.

Salty Snacks: Pork rinds, Potato chips, Salty pretzels, popcorn, trail mix, salty almonds, salty crackers, cheese doodles, tortilla chips, with cheese snacks, snack mix, tater tots, etc.

Salted Canned and Jarred Products: Most canned and ready made soups and broths, marinated artichoke hearts, salted canned corn and additional vegetables, refried beans, spam, pickles, cocktail onions, canned chili, olives, jarred franks, etc.

Examples of lunch meats and cold cuts include sausage, bacon, hot dogs, and more.

Frozen Dinners: Frozen pizza, frozen meals, frozen prepared lasagna, frozen Chinese cuisine dishes, frozen pot pies, etc.

Salty Packaged Side Dishes: Stuffing mixes, instant mashed potatoes, macaroni and cheese, rice mixtures, pilaf, hash browns, etc.

Salty Dairy Products:

Dairy products with a salty flavor include Parmesan cheese, processed hard cheeses, buttermilk, feta cheese, cottage cheese, sour cream, cream cheese, and brie.

Bread products with a salty flavor include canned and prepared biscuits and croissants, muffin mixes, various pancakes and waffle mixes, Danishes,

English muffins, protein pizza dough, tortillas and wraps, croutons, hot dog buns, and dinner rolls, instant oatmeal, certain boxed cereals, salted bagels, salty crackers, and pita chips.

Examples of sauces and condiments include Soy sauce, salsa, teriyaki sauce, spicy sauce, barbecue sauce, sauerkraut, some types of salad dressings, most tomato sauces, and salted peanut butter., etc.

Drinks: Vegetable juice and salty alcoholic drinks, certain hot chocolate powders, etc.

Salt is an ingredient in many salted seasoning mixes, including table salt, garlic salt, onion salt, MSG, and meat tenderizers. etc.

Restaurant Foods: Soups, broths, appetizers, pizza, entrees. Aim for meals tagged as "heart-healthy" or "lower-sodium" alternatives or ask if your dish may be made with minimum salt.

Fats and Oils: Salted butter, margarine, olio, lard, cutting, bacon fat, etc.

Similar High-Sodium Items: Anything containing over 20% of the daily amount of sodium.

Foods to Eat On a Low-Sodium Diet

A low-sodium diet should contain as many whole, unprocessed healthful foods such as vegetables, fruits, legumes, and lean proteins as possible with judicious selections of low-sodium dairy products, nuts, seeds, etc.

Herbs and unsalted spices ought to be used rather than high-sodium prepackaged sauces and seasoning blends. The following are things to consume on a low-sodium diet:

Vegetables: Fresh or frozen kale, carrots, lettuce Swiss chard, broccoli, zucchini, cucumbers, onions, cauliflower, asparagus, sweet potatoes, beets, squash, onions, etc. Resist canned spinach and other canned veggies, since they are highly salty.

Fruits: A variety of fruits including pears, apples, melons, oranges, grapefruit, plums, apricots, peaches, berries, bananas, pomegranates, kiwi, coconut, tomatoes, dates, figs, and more can be found.

Whole Grains and Bread Products: Whole, untreated oats, whole wheat, barley, brown rice, quinoa, teff, farro, etc; low-sodium cereals, low-sodium bread, unsalted pretzels and crackers, plain rice, pasta, etc.

Lean Meats, Poultry, and Fish: Unsalted either fresh or frozen lean beef, bison, deer, hog, chicken, turkey, salmon, scallops, tofu, unsalted or low-sodium canned tuna, etc.

Low-Sodium Dairy Products: Generally, low-sodium dairy products include Swiss cheese, goat cheese, ricotta, fresh mozzarella, cottage cheese with no sodium added, milk, and eggs.

Legumes: Clean canned legumes, such as dry or low-sodium beans, lentils, peas, peanuts, soy, etc., to reduce the sodium content.

Nuts and Seeds: Unsalted or slightly salted almonds, pistachios, walnuts, cashews, pecans, chia seeds, flax seeds, pumpkin seeds, sesame seeds, hemp seeds, sunflower seeds, macadamia nuts, Brazil nuts, unsalted peanut butter, etc.

Examples of **Fats and Oils** include Olive oil, avocados, flaxseed oil, coconut oil, unsalted butter, and more.

Herbs & Spices: Basil, thyme, pepper, cinnamon, clove, nutmeg, ginger, rosemary, cumin, unsalted chili powder, etc.

Beverages: A variety of beverages, such as water, herbal tea, green tea, black tea, red wine, and coffee.

Sample Low-Sodium Diet Meal Plan

Wondering what a day of eating may look like on a low-sodium diet? Below, we give an example low-sodium diet meal plan:

Breakfast: Mix one cup of plain Greek yogurt, half a cup of mixed berries, half a cup of muesli or low-fat granola, blueberries, raspberries, and unsweetened coconut flakes for a delicious snack.

Lunch: Rice dish prepared with brown rice, baked chicken breast, avocado, tomatoes, cilantro, low-sodium cheese, lime juice, jalapeño, and unsalted almonds.

Snack: Melon and unsalted almonds.

Dinner: Grilled salmon over cauliflower rice seasoned containing lemon juice and finely chopped parsley, baked sweet potato with Greek yogurt or unsalted butter, spinach salad with tomatoes, cucumbers, and carrots, and low-sodium vinaigrette.

Snack: Apple with unsalted almond butter dusted with cinnamon and one ounce of dark chocolate.

9.2 Grocery Shopping Tips

1. Plan your meals: Take the time to plan out your meals for the week, taking into mind the number of low-sodium, low-carb items that you will require. This will allow you to know what to purchase and will also help keep your shopping cost in control.

2. Study nutrition labels: Before buying any item, take the time to study the nutrition labels. Look for goods that are low in salt and carbs. Pay attention to serving sizes and the quantity of salt and carbs in each dish.

3. Buy fresh produce: Fresh vegetables and fruits are naturally low in sodium and carbs. Try to purchase organic wherever feasible to limit your exposure to pesticides. Buy in bulk when you can to save money.

4. Pick lean proteins: Lean proteins are an excellent source of low-sodium, low-carb nourishment. Look for slim pieces of meat such as chicken breast, fish, and turkey. Also, seek low-sodium canned tuna, salmon, and sardines.

5. Limit processed foods: Processed meals are often rich in salt and carbs. Avoid things such as canned soups, frozen meals, and packaged dinners.

6. Stock up on spices: Spices may be a terrific way to add taste to your dish without adding salt and sugar. Look for herbs, spices, and seasonings that are low in salt.

7. Go for low-sodium spices: Look for low-sodium spices such as mustard, salsa, vinegar, and low-sodium dressings.

8. Check out the health food section: The health food aisle may be a terrific source of low-sodium and low-carb goods. Look for goods such as low-sodium crackers, almonds, and granola bars.

9. Drink water: Water is the greatest beverage to pick when attempting to lower your salt and carbohydrate consumption. Avoid sugary drinks and beverages that are rich in salt.

10. Never forget about snacks: Snacks are an essential element of a balanced diet. Look for low-sodium and low-carb snacks such as unsalted almonds, plain popcorn, and fruit.

These ideas might help you make healthier and more educated decisions while grocery shopping.

By following these suggestions, you can make sure that you are receiving the nourishment you need without ingesting too much salt or carbs.

9.3 Stocking Your Pantry

1. **Whole Grains:** Whole grains are an essential element of a low-sodium, low-carb diet. Whole grains such as quinoa, oats, and barley are filled with minerals and are low in salt and carbohydrates. Keep a variety of nutritious grains in your cupboard so you may mix and match them in your meals.

2. **Legumes:** Legumes such as lentils, beans, and peas are excellent sources of protein and fiber and are lower in salt and carbohydrates. They may be used in soups and salads, as a side dish, or as a main entrée.

3. **Nuts and Seeds:** Nuts and seeds are a terrific source of healthy fats, protein, and fiber, and are low in salt and carbohydrates. Keep a variety of nuts and seeds in your cupboard, such as almonds, walnuts, cashews, pumpkin seeds, and sunflower seeds.

4. **Herbs and Spices:** Herbs and spices are a terrific method to add flavor to your foods without adding salt. Keep a variety of herbs and spices in your cupboard to add flavor to your foods without adding salt or carbohydrates.

5. Canned veggies: Canned veggies are a terrific way to add vegetables to your meals without adding salt or carbohydrates. Try to seek low-sodium or no-salt-added options.

6. Low-Sodium Broth: Low-sodium broth is a terrific method to add flavor to your foods without adding sodium. Look for low-sodium options or prepare your broth.

7. Low-Sugar Condiments: Condiments such as ketchup, mustard, and salsa may add flavor to your food without adding too many carbohydrates or salt. Look for low-sugar versions or prepare your condiments.

8. Olive Oil and Vinegar: Olive oil and vinegar are a terrific way to add flavor to your foods without adding carbohydrates or salt. Keep a selection of olive oils and vinegar in your cupboard so you may mix and match them in your recipes.

9. Low-salt Canned Fish: Canned fish like tuna, salmon, and sardines are a wonderful source of protein and omega-3 fatty acids, and are low in salt and carbohydrates. Make careful to seek low-sodium versions.

10. **Low-Carb Flour:** Low-carb flour is a terrific way to add texture and taste to your foods without adding too many carbohydrates. Try to opt for low-carb versions such as almond flour or coconut flour.

11. **Coconut Milk:** Coconut milk is a terrific way to add richness to your recipes without adding too many carbohydrates. Try to hunt for low-sugar options or prepare your own.

12. **Low-Carb Sweeteners**: Low-carb sweeteners such as stevia, monk fruit, and erythritol is a terrific way to add sweetness to your foods without adding too many carbohydrates. Look for low-carb versions or build your own.

13. **Edamame**: Edamame is a fantastic source of protein and fiber and is low in salt and carbohydrates. Keep a package of frozen edamame in your freezer for a simple snack or side dish.

14. Cauliflower Rice: Cauliflower rice is a terrific way to add texture and taste to your recipes without adding too many carbohydrates. Keep a package of frozen cauliflower rice in your freezer for a simple side dish.

15. Avocado: Avocado is an excellent source of beneficial fats and is low in salt and carbohydrates. Keep a couple of avocados in your cupboard for a simple snack or side dish.

CHAPTER 10

Conclusion

10.1 Reflection on Low Sodium Low Carb Cooking

My experience on low salt low carb cooking has been an eye-opening one. With so numerous diets out there, it may be tough to find one that is nutritious, sustainable, and pleasant.

Low salt low carb cooking has done all of these things for me. Not only have I been able to enjoy delectable meals without feeling restricted, but I have also been able to discover a way to eat properly.

The first step in my quest was to minimize my salt consumption by removing processed meals and eating more natural foods.

I was astonished to learn that several delectable selections were both low in salt and low in carbohydrates.

I was able to uncover recipes that employed fresh herbs and spices to bring out the natural tastes of the meal. I also made sure to incorporate loads of veggies to get the most out of my meals.

I was also able to experiment with various cooking methods to make sure I was getting the most out of my meals.

Grilling and roasting veggies brought out their inherent sweetness and made them more delightful to consume.

Steaming and boiling veggies was a terrific method to keep them low in salt and low in carbohydrates.

My journey with cookbook proved to be great. I am now more conscious of the significance of minimizing processed meals, eating more natural foods, and exploring new cooking ways to make food more delightful.

Also more careful of the salt and carb levels of the food I consume, and I have discovered methods to make my meals nutritious and enjoyable.

It is essential to remember that low-sodium and low-carb cooking can be pleasurable and gratifying, and it doesn't have to be a sacrifice.

With a little bit of ingenuity and experimenting, it is possible to produce tasty and healthful meals.

Reflecting on my experience with low-salt low-carb cooking has taught me to become more careful about my dietary choices.

I now have a greater knowledge of the significance of minimizing processed meals, eating more whole foods, and exploring alternate cooking ways that make food more delightful.

I now have a greater awareness of the need of managing salt and carb levels in my meals to make sure I am getting the most out of my diet.

Overall, low-sodium low-carb cooking has been a terrific journey for me and I look forward to continuing to enhance my knowledge and abilities in the kitchen. *I know it will be same for you as you read and try out in the kitchen all the amazing recipes in this book.*

10.2 Final Thoughts

It's astonishing how little people truly know about salt, fat and carbohydrates, given these three ingredients are crucial portions of a balanced diet.

Fat and oils should be regulated when it comes to how much you consume every day, but they're still useful and crucial.

As with so many things, decisions need to be made regarding how much and the sorts of fats and oils you eat.

For example, lighter oils may be used for cooking, and unsaturated fats, rather than saturated, should be utilized.

But why are fats and carbohydrates and oils vital in the diet? The body derives energy from these elements as well as utilizes them to carry additional nutrients like vitamins A, D, E, K, and components known as carotenoids.

Fats also operate as building blocks for specific membranes and tissues in the body and are necessary for many of their functions.

Severely reducing fat consumption may be detrimental; many experts advocate keeping it to fewer than 20% of one's daily calories but again, balance is important.

Only a doctor can suggest whether you should cut your fat intake to anything less than this.

And the sort of fat you intake is also a role. Trans fats, saturated fats, and anything that may elevate your cholesterol levels are not good.

These items have been connected with an increased risk of heart attacks, heart disease, stroke, and other cardiovascular disorders.

And of course, being overweight is also related to a diet heavy in these kinds of fats.

Most specialists believe that the worst fats to eat are saturated fats and trans fats. Saturated oils are fats that become solid at ambient temperature and normally are what you would call animal fats.

So, butter would be such a fat. The fat in meals that are animal products such as bacon grease would also be classified as saturated fat.

Cholesterol often originates from meals that are also rich in animal fats, such as red meat and eggs. And note that dairy foods are derived from animal fats, so be cautious about ice cream, whole milk, and so on.

Sometimes it's easy to overlook the fatty amounts of meals because of how food labels are worded.

Often it becomes tricky how they categorize fats; generally, processed foods will include a high degree of trans fats.

There are nonetheless certain fats that are healthier alternatives for you.

These are termed polyunsaturated fats and monounsaturated fats. These might be present in things like olive oil and canola oil.

Many refer to them as "lighter" oils and utilizing them in your cooking will aid you with better choices and a healthier diet overall.

These fats are also liquid at room temperature, so keep that in mind while thinking about how to identify the difference.

Some even feel that these fats have therapeutic qualities to them!

There are even fats that are excellent for you and that tend to encourage good health. These may contain Omega-3 fatty acids as found in fish.

Some claim they even reduce cholesterol levels!

But what about carbohydrates? These too are part of a balanced diet since they supply energy and other necessary elements.

These are present in fresh fruits and vegetables as well as in goods like dairy products and whole grains.

However, like fats, not all carbs are the same and some are not as beneficial for you as others.

Whole grains are normally the carbs you want to pick. When picking slices of bread and cereals, select ones that include whole grains and avoid those that are refined, meaning processed into white flour.

It's also smart to be aware of the quantity of sugar you intake, and this involves not only sweets but also drinks and sugary pastries.

When you consume things like this, you're taking in a lot of calories for not a lot of foods and this might entail being overweight and having difficulties with your blood sugar and other similar health concerns.

There are two usual ingredients that many individuals take too much of, and this would be salt and sugar.

Salt of course is needed for optimal nutrition but too much salt is hazardous, and many individuals take much too much of it.

This may lead to high blood pressure, holding water, and other major health risks.

However, if you pick low-sodium meals and put away the salt shaker you may discover that you may prevent these and other health risks.

Dear Reader

THANK YOU

Made in the USA
Monee, IL
13 March 2024

55000151R00085